Marseille
Travel Guide

Quick Trips Series

No part of this publication may be reproduced, stored in a retrieval system, or transmitted, in any form or by any means without the prior written permission of the publisher, nor be otherwise circulated in any form of binding or cover other than that in which it is published and without similar condition being imposed on the subsequent purchaser. If there are any errors or omissions in copyright acknowledgements the publisher will be pleased to insert the appropriate acknowledgement in any subsequent printing of this publication. Although we have taken all reasonable care in researching this book we make no warranty about the accuracy or completeness of its content and disclaim all liability arising from its use.

Copyright © 2016, Astute Press
All Rights Reserved.

Table of Contents

MARSEILLE — 5
- Customs & Culture 6
- Geography 8
- Weather & Best Time to Visit 10

SIGHTS & ACTIVITIES: WHAT TO SEE & DO — 12
- Unité d'Habitation 12
- La Place Castellane 14
- Calanque de Morgiou 15
- Le Cours Julien 17
- Museum of Mediterranean Archaeology 18
- Notre Dame de la Garde 19
- Le Vieux Port (Old Port) 21
- Château d'If 23
- Panier 25
- Parc Balneaire du Prado 27
- Petit Train Marseille 29
- Ferry Boat Ride 30
- Palais & Parc Longchamp 31
- L'Estaque 33

BUDGET TIPS — 35

- **Accommodation** 35
  - Hotel La Résidence du Vieux Port Marseille 35
  - Best Western La Joliette 36
  - Music Hotel 37
  - Hotel Lutia 37
  - Ibis Gare Saint Charles 38
- **Restaurants, Cafés & Bars** 38
  - Four des Navettes 39
  - L'Escapade Marseillaise 40
  - Le Julien 40
  - The Cup of Tea 41
  - La Brocéliande 41
- **Shopping** 42
  - Le Centre Commercial les Puces 42
  - The Market at Noailles (Le Marché de Noailles) 43
  - Prado Market 44
  - La Chocolatière du Panier 44
  - Centre Bourse 45

KNOW BEFORE YOU GO — 47

- **Entry Requirements** 47
- **Health Insurance** 48
- **Travelling with Pets** 48
- **Airports** 49
- **Airlines** 51
- **Currency** 52
- **Banking & ATMs** 52
- **Credit Cards** 52
- **Tourist Taxes** 53
- **Reclaiming VAT** 53
- **Tipping Policy** 54

- **Mobile Phones** 54
- **Dialling Code** 55
- **Emergency Numbers** 55
- **Time Zone** 56
- **Daylight Savings Time** 57
- **School Holidays** 57
- **Driving Laws** 57
- **Drinking Laws** 58
- **Smoking Laws** 59
- **Electricity** 59
- **Food & Drink** 60

MARSEILLE TRAVEL GUIDE

Marseille

Marseille is the second most populous city in France and has the largest port on the Mediterranean. Located close to the tourist resorts of the French Riviera, Marseille is the economic centre of the Provence/Alps/Côte d'Azur region.

Marseille's location opposite North Africa is reflected in its ambience, noticeable when visiting sites like the colorful

MARSEILLE TRAVEL GUIDE

Noailles market. Marseille is quite different to the larger Paris. Without the language similarities, you may even think you are in another country. Marseille's cliffs, fjords (clanques), sea views, beaches and harbors define the city. The city's port welcomes over 2 million visitors per year.

Cruise ships bring passengers to the city as well so that they can enjoy not only the beach scene, but also its history, museums, theaters, and architecture.

🌍 Customs & Culture

Marseille is one of the oldest cities in Europe, founded in 600 B.C. by the Phoceans. Its population of 1 million is a melting pot of culture. Besides its French citizens, a number of Spanish and Italians who immigrated to the city after World War II have also left their mark on the city.

MARSEILLE TRAVEL GUIDE

This diversity is also apparent when visiting its incredible restaurants and cafes.

It is this diverse culture that the city celebrates regularly with its many festivals throughout the year. One of the most popular is the Avec le Temps, taking place in springtime at Espace Julien: one of Marseille's concert halls. Avec le Temps showcases and celebrates native French artists who represent all different types of music. Moving toward the end of June, La Fête Bleue (The Blue Festival) is celebrated annually. This is a festival during which entertainment in all forms is offered with the theme being the color blue, as the name states.

Also in June, toward the end of the month, is La Fête du Panier; as it offers shows, concerts and different shopping experiences in the oldest part of the city. Another popular

MARSEILLE TRAVEL GUIDE

festival in Marseille that lasts all summer is Le FDAmM or Festival de Danse et des Arts Multiples de Marseille. Le FDAmM is an art festival, primarily dance, which exists as a way for artists to gain exposure within the city.

Heading into September is the ten-year-old music festival known as Marsatac. There is also a World Music festival known as La Fiesta Des Duds, held at Dock des Suds in October. Besides music, Marseille also celebrates the holidays, as exhibited during La Foire aux Santons. This is a popular Christmas market that is held near Vieux Port from late November through December.

🌍 Geography

Marseille is located on the Mediterranean Sea in the middle of the French Riviera. A wide boulevard called, the Canebière, cuts through the city as it starts at Vieux Port

MARSEILLE TRAVEL GUIDE

(the Old Port) and stretches east toward the Réformés quarter. In the Bay of Marseille, are four islands that compose the Frioul Archipelago.

About 30 km from the city is its airport, Marseille-Provence International Airport. From the airport, visitors can access Marseille by bus, taxi, or train. The main train station is St. Charles, which is within walking distance to the Old Port and Canebière. The train station is accessible by bus or by two subway lines. The bus station is right next to the train station.

Getting to Marseille from other French cities is quite easy. However, once arriving in the city, do not be intimidated or discouraged by its public transportation. It is actually encouraged to use, since driving in the center of the city can be torturous. If you are driving into the city center, be

MARSEILLE TRAVEL GUIDE

sure to park it in a reputable location and switch to public transportation. Subways operate until 10:30 p.m. except on weekends when they close at 12:30 a.m.

Trams run until 12:30 a.m. seven days per week. Busses, however, stop operating around 9:00 p.m. usually. If you are on a bus route and need to get somewhere after 9:00 p.m., be ready to take a taxi.

A good way to reach Marseille is by ferry and this is an attraction in itself. It crosses the Vieux Port (the Old Port) and is known as the shortest boat ride in Europe. Since Marseille is a large city, visitors should be aware that there are certain areas to avoid, as is the case in most large cities. Smart tourists wear money belts and avoid carrying anything of too much value.

It is advisable to avoid many of the northern neighborhoods at night, as well as Gare St. Charles. Also, if driving a car, be sure to keep the doors locked. The city center is quite congested and people on motorbikes have been known to open car doors with the driver inside, while quickly snatching purses and valuables and then speeding away. This does not mean that you should be paranoid, however. Marseille is generally a safe city. Just be smart and aware of your surroundings.

🌍 Weather & Best Time to Visit

Marseille's climate is a typical Mediterranean one with warm, dry summers and humid, mild winters. Its coldest months are December through February when the temperatures are an average 54 °F (12 °C). Its warmest months, like in most cities in Europe, are July and August when temperatures average 86 °F (30 °C).

MARSEILLE TRAVEL GUIDE

During the winter and spring, Marseille experiences the Mistral, a cold and bitter wind that originates in the Rhône valley. Its proximity to the Sahara Desert also means that it can experience a Sirocco, a warm wind that carries sand from Africa, across the Mediterranean.

Summertime is obviously the most popular time to visit Marseille, since this is when most people take their vacations. However, its warm climate is generally nice all year round.

If you want to experience the warmer weather while avoiding the crowds, plan your visit during late spring or early autumn. Definitely avoid Marseille in July if you do not like crowds. This is when the entire country celebrates Bastille Day. In Marseille, the festivities last approximately

MARSEILLE TRAVEL GUIDE

two weeks and are quite exciting with plenty of entertainment to keep revelers happy.

Sights & Activities: What to See & Do

 Unité d'Habitation

280 Bd Michelet

13008 Marseille France

MARSEILLE TRAVEL GUIDE

+33 491 16 7800

http://www.marseille-citeradieuse.org/

As a product of modern urban architect, Le Corbusier, Unité d'Habitation is also known as "the house of the foolish" (la maison du fada). By others more optimistic, it is referred to as, "the radiant city."

The building represents the architect's dedication to improving living conditions for residents of crowded cities. He felt that people need to feel part of a community in order to be a successful and productive social unit. Without a close-knit community, people feel too scattered to have a connection. And furthermore, without this connection, people fail to respect each other.

MARSEILLE TRAVEL GUIDE

So by offering housing units, such as the Unité d'Habitation, Le Corbusier was able to test this theory. Although people who reside in his housing units live in separate dwellings; the building has a communal shopping area, church, and school for children of the community. There is also a bar and restaurant on the third floor. Between 10 a.m. and 6 p.m., visitors can access the roof where there is a stunning view of the sea and hills that surround Marseille.

The huge roof terrace of the building has magnificent panoramic views. Recently, it was taken over by designer, Ito Morabito; who also goes by the name, Ora Ïto. He bought the 6,500 square foot (600 meter) in 2010. Originally designed to be a gymnasium, it has recently been restored with plans for a bookshop, café, and exhibition space.

🌐 La Place Castellane

Intersection of Boulevard Baille,

Avenue du Prado and Rue de Rome

La Place Castellane is actually a roundabout at the intersection of Boulevard Baille, Rue de Rome, and Avenue du Prado. In the middle, there is a fountain and sculpture, difficult to miss with its tall column erupting from the center.

La Place Castellane is not so much an attraction but a location that serves as a meeting point before heading to one of the many cafes and cinemas that surround it. It is named after Marquis de Castellane-Majastre who donated the land and financed the project.

There are two metro lines, numbers one and two, which service La Place Castellane. Be sure not to confuse La Place Castellane with La Castellane. The latter is one of the poor suburbs of Marseille.

🌐 Calanque de Morgiou

The Calanques are a collective group of small fjords that are located south of Marseille, near Cassis. The view is stunning with a clear blue sea set below limestone cliffs. Whether you view the Calanques from the sea or from the cliffs, you are sure to get incredible views. Just keep in mind that the hike up the cliffs can be quite arduous. The trail leading up to the Calanques (GR) is marked with white and red stripes and is easy to find.

Although all of the fjords offer a great view, the Calanque de Morgiou is the largest of them. It was formerly a fishing

MARSEILLE TRAVEL GUIDE

port when tuna fishing was popular during the 17th century. The fishing cabins still exist today but they are used for tourism purposes instead of for fishing.

Another reason for the popularity of the Calanque de Morgiou is the Cosquer cave. This is an underwater grotto with multiple cave drawings that date back over 27,000 years.

To reach Calanque de Morgiou, you can either take a boat or a bus. Different tour companies offer boat access. If taking the bus, take the #21 bus to the University campus at Luminy. The busses to Luminy leave from Vieux Port and Rond Point du Prado. The ride to Luminy takes only about 20 minutes. Once there, a 15 minute walk takes you to a location where you have the choice to head up to a lookout point or down to the Clanque. If you head up, the walk is approximately 20 minutes along a ridge. The descent takes about a half hour.

These are the two most popular options and you can see people coming and going throughout the day when the weather is warm. There are other options for those more adventurous as well. Be sure to bring water for your hike as well as your bathing suit should you care to swim in the beautiful water below. Also, be aware that some of the Calanques may be closed from the months of June to September when there can be a high fire risk.

🌐 Le Cours Julien

http://coursjulien.marsnet.org/

The Cours Julien is a partially pedestrianized road in the 6th arrondissement. The neighborhood is composed of

MARSEILLE TRAVEL GUIDE

artists, musicians, and free spirits. Before 1970, farmers would congregate in the main courtyard to sell their produce. Now it serves as a beautiful garden that transforms into a pedestrian zone with attractive fountains and garden greenery. It is a trendy area with theaters, concert halls, bars and restaurants abundant.

What makes Le Cours Julien interesting is that it is situated right in the middle of the hustle and bustle of the city. Its car-free zones, laid back mood, and general quaintness seem to be protesting against the big city vibe. It is easily accessible, only a 15 minute walk from the Vieux Port. If making a visit to the area, try to avoid Sundays and Mondays when restaurants and shops tend to be closed.

MARSEILLE TRAVEL GUIDE

🌐 Museum of Mediterranean Archaeology

Centre de la Vieille Charité, 2 Rue de la Charité

+33 491 14 5880

http://www.muselia.com/france/marseille/museum-of-mediterranean-archaeology/2979

The Museum of Mediterranean Archaeology is one of the oldest museums in Marseille. From its establishment in 1863 until 1989, its home was Château Borély before moving to the Vieille Charité building.

Although the museum houses other tenants, the museum occupies most of the first floor. It is within these walls where you can find an overview of the ancient civilizations that once occupied the banks of the Mediterranean Sea,

MARSEILLE TRAVEL GUIDE

including one of the largest collections of Egyptological artifacts in France.

There is a separate area dedicated to Cyprus, Etruria, Rome, and Greece. Another area is devoted to Mediterranean prehistory from 1 A.D. until the 7th century. With Marseille's long history under Greek rule, visitors are allowed to see a glimpse of the everyday life of the Greek people who lived in the region centuries ago.

To get to the museum by metro, get off at the Joliette stop. The museum is open daily from 10 a.m. until 5 p.m.

🌑 Notre Dame de la Garde

Rue Fort du Sanctuaire, 13006

+33 491 13 4080

http://www.notredamedelagarde.com/

MARSEILLE TRAVEL GUIDE

Notre Dame de la Garde (meaning Our Lady of the Guard) is a famous Catholic Basilica in Marseille. This Neo-Byzantine-style church was built by architect, Henri-Jacques Espérandieu and touches the sky above Marseille as it sits 490 feet (149 meters) high on a hill south of Vieux Port.

Every year on Assumption day, August 15th, people make the pilgrimage to this church that dates back to the 13th century. Residents of Marseille consider Notre-Dame de la Garde as a protector and guardian of the city. It is also sometimes called "the good mother" (la bonne mère).

Although the Basilica dates back to the year 1214, the current building is actually a replacement of the original. There is a lower church (or crypt) carved from rock,

MARSEILLE TRAVEL GUIDE

Romanesque style, as well as a Neo-Byzantine style upper church which is decorated by mosaics. From outside the church, you'll notice a 135 foot (41 meter) square bell tower, a 42 foot (12.5 meter) belfry, and a 27 foot (11.2 meter) statue of the Madonna and Child made of copper and gold leaf.

During the years between 2001 and 2008, the Basilica went through an extensive restoration. This was due to the effects of candle smoke on the mosaics, as well as bullets from World War II during the liberation of France. It has also been discovered that the limestone that was used to build the Basilica is sensitive to atmospheric corrosion.

From March to September, the Basilica observes summer hours and offers mass on Sundays at 8 a.m., 9 a.m., 10 a.m., 11 a.m., noon, and 5 p.m. The 9 a.m. and 11 a.m. masses are in the crypt. On weekdays, mass takes place in the crypt at 7:25 a.m., 9 a.m., and 5 p.m. in the crypt. On Saturdays, it takes place at 5 p.m. in the Basilica.

From October 1st through April 1st, the Basilica observes winter hours and offers mass on Sundays at 8 a.m., 9 a.m., 10 a.m., 11 a.m., noon, and 4:30 p.m. The 9 a.m. and 11 a.m. masses are in the crypt. On weekdays, mass takes place in the crypt at 7:25 a.m., 9 a.m., and 4:30 p.m. in the crypt. On Saturdays, it takes place at 4:30 p.m. in the Basilica.

🌐 Le Vieux Port (Old Port)

Le Vieux Port (or Old Port) is located at the end of the Canebière, the historic main street that runs through the old quarter of Marseille. It is the natural harbor of the city

MARSEILLE TRAVEL GUIDE

as well as the center of the city, even if not geographically. This is where everything happens.

The history of the Old Port dates back to 600 BC when Greeks from Phocaea landed there by ship. They set up a trading post and it is still used as a marketplace today as people enjoy watching the fishermen auction off their catches of the day. During the Middle Ages, cannabis was grown in order to produce rope for the mariners and fishermen. This is where the name, Canebière, originated.

Unfortunately, much of the Old Port is not so old after all. Since it was left in ruins during World War II's Battle of Marseille, much of it had to be reconstructed. Today, the Old Port still serves as a marina, a stop for cruise ships and local boat trips, as well as a thriving fish market.

MARSEILLE TRAVEL GUIDE

A huge rejuvenation project recently revamped the Port since it was designated as the 2013 European Capital of Culture. It is for this reason that the Old Port may be a bit more popular now amongst tourists than ever before. When visiting the port, it may be best to avoid having an itinerary. Since it is closed off to vehicles, it is a great place to simply walk around and absorb the sights, sounds, and flavors that the area has to offer.

🌐 Château d'If

Embarcadère Frioul If,

1 Quai de la Fraternité

+33 496 11 0350

http://www.if.monuments-nationaux.fr/

Located on the island of If, the smallest of the islands in the Frioul Archipelago, is the Château d'If. Despite being

MARSEILLE TRAVEL GUIDE

referred to as a château, it has been used as both a fortress and a prison. It was made famous by the popular novel by Alexandre Dumas, *The Count of Monte Cristo*.

The island itself spans 11 square miles (30 square kilometers) and is uninhabited apart from the château. Slightly intimidating, the château is a three story building, square shaped, with walls that are 90 feet long (28 meters) on each side. Three gun towers stand guard the way they did in 1524 when King Francis I chose the island for its strategic location for protection from sea attacks.

Château d'If may have been a better prison than a fortress. Its dangerous currents and remote location made it virtually escape-proof and one of the most feared prisons in France. Despite the characters escaping from the prison in the book, The Count of Monte Cristo; no one

MARSEILLE TRAVEL GUIDE

has ever really escaped. Still, visitors to the prison can find cells named after the two characters: Edmond Dantès and Abbé Faria.

The château was used as a prison until the end of the 19th century and was opened to the public in 1890. It is now a popular tourist destination and can be reached by boat from the Old Port.

From May 16th through September 16th, Château d'If is open daily from 9:30 am until 6:10 p.m.

From September 17th through March 31st, it is open every day but Mondays from 9:30 a.m. until 4:45 p.m. From April 1st through May 15th, it is open daily from 9:30 a.m. until 4:45 p.m.

MARSEILLE TRAVEL GUIDE

Adult admission is 5,50 €. Children under 18 are free.

Boats leave from the Old Port. Schedules are available on the Frioul If Express website.

 Panier

(Neighborhood to the north of the Old Port)

Just north of the Old Port is a neighborhood with tall and narrow houses sat amongst steep steps and wash lines: Panier. This is the oldest part of Marseille and is steeped in history. This is where the Greeks first settled when they arrived in the city in 600 BC.

MARSEILLE TRAVEL GUIDE

Since then, a variety of immigrants followed. The area's name comes from a 17th century inn called, Le Logis du Panier. Panier means "basket" in French.

Unfortunately, just like the Old Port, Panier was not immune to the effects of World War II. Although some antiquity has survived, post-war architecture is visible, mainly in the form of granite apartment blocks that divide Panier from the Old Port. Still, it maintains its vibrant diversity that was established by immigrants centuries ago.

Depending on your personality, you may want to either avoid or flock to Panier during the midde to end of June. This is when France's biggest street party occurs: Fête du Panier, taking place on or near midsummer's night.

MARSEILLE TRAVEL GUIDE

Community events and children's shows commence the festivities during the afternoon hours. The party heads into the evening with plenty of live, world music and a unique atmosphere. You can wander the street stalls, sampling a culinary tour of the different ethnicities that exist within the community.

Many parts of the Panier are pedestrian-only after 11:30 a.m. with the exception of the Petit Train. An attraction in itself, it makes one Panier stop: at the Vieille Charité. This is an old monument in the middle of the neighborhood that hosts different exhibitions from time to time.

There is also an informative self-guided walking tour to be followed by the plaques set in the ground at various locations. There is no need to follow a strict itinerary, however. Simply allow yourself a couple hours to stroll around, possibly stopping in a gallery or shopping for local crafts.

To get to the Panier, simply walk north from the Old Port. Or catch the Petit Train, for a guided tour.

🌐 Parc Balneaire du Prado

Promenade Georges Pompidou

+33 491 55 2551

Created from the land excavated after making Marseille's metro in 1970, is man-made beach area, Parc Balnéaire du Prado. The 1 km long beach is actually five separate beaches that start at the city center and span five kilometers south. The names of the beaches from north to south are Plage du Prado Nord, Plage du Prado Sud,

MARSEILLE TRAVEL GUIDE

Plage Borély, Plage Bonneveine, and Plage Vieille Chapelle.

Although the quality of the water is dependent upon other factors and sometimes not of the best swimming quality, the beaches themselves are quite nice. They have showers, public toilets, first aid stations, lifeguards, and free lockers for those who want to keep their valuables safe while enjoying the beach scene. There is a children's playground at Borély and Prado du Nord. Borély and Bonneveine both have lounge chairs and umbrellas available to rent.

The popluar Fête du Vent takes place at these beaches every September. This is a festival that pays homage to the otherwise cursed Mistral wind (a hot wind that blows north from Africa). It is celebrated with hundreds of colored kites flying over the Mediterranean. On an annual basis, more than 100,000 people visit the festival.

One common way to get to Parc Balneaire du Prado is to take bus #83 which you can catch at the Old Port and take straight to the start of the park.

🌎 Petit Train Marseille

176 Quai du Port

+33 491 25 2469

http://www.petit-train-marseille.com/

Marseille's Petit Train (little train) is a fun way to see the city. You will recognize it when you see it, with its distinct white and blue colors, resembling a toy train of sorts. The train has a few routes from which to choose.

MARSEILLE TRAVEL GUIDE

Route 1 goes to Notre Dame de la Garde. It starts at the Old Port and leads through the Corniche seafront and then up to the basilica where you can observe stunning views of the city from above. During high season (April through November), the train departs every 20 minutes, daily. During low season (December through March), the train runs every half hour, daily. The cost during high season is 8 €. During low season, it is 7 €. Children ages 3 – 11 are always 4 €.

Another route called "Le Vieux Marseille" (The Old Marseille), takes you to the old parts of the city with a few different hotel and museum stops. This is the route that takes visitors to the Panier. This route operates daily from April 1st through November 15th, with trains leaving every 30 minutes. The cost during the month of April is 6 €.

After May 1st, it is 7 €. Children ages 3 – 11 are always 3 €.

The third route is the Friuli route which leaves from Port Friuli on Ratonneau Island. It operates during high season from June 15th through September 1st, with trains leaving every 30 minute. The cost is 4 € for adults and 2 € for children ages 3 – 11.

🌐 Ferry Boat Ride

Marseille's ferry boats are not only a mode of transportation but an attraction as well. The service, which crosses the Old Port every few minutes, is entirely free of cost. You can catch the ferry between the Rive Neuve and the Town Hall (La Mairie). Although it is fairly new, commencing in 2010, it has seen its share of technical problems. For this reason, it is frequently out of service.

However, there are other options for crossing the port, which include the historic ferry boat, César.

There is also an option that is not free, but not too expensive either, at 3 € for a 40 minute trip. It is a new fast boat called the batobus, or navette. They run once per hour and leave from the same stop as the Château d'If at the Old Port.

🌍 Palais & Parc Longchamp

Boulevard du Jardin Zoologique

Despite its name, Palais Longchamp is not a palace at all. It is a monument created in celebration of the construction of the Marseille canal which brought water from the Durance River to an otherwise dry Marseille.

MARSEILLE TRAVEL GUIDE

One wouldn't think such a city on the sea would have water shortages, but it only receives an average of two rainy days per month during the high part of summer. It is for this reason that a monument was devoted to a much appreciated canal at a volatile time in the 19th century.

Not only did the canal supply a water source, but it also connected the city to the rest of the national waterways. This opened up important trading routes.

The canal is 50 miles (80 km) long with over 10 of those miles underground. It took 15 years to complete before being opened in 1849. It was used as a primary water source since 1970. Now it stands as a glorious monument to the appreciation for the element of water with its fountains, columns, staircases and arches.

The Parc Longchamp surrounds the monument which sits in a suburb east of Saint Charles Station. The park is a beautiful sight alone as well.

🌍 L'Estaque

Just west of Marseille is a town known as L'Estaque. In French (Provençal), L'Estaque means "the mooring that attaches boats to the wharf." It became a manufacturing town during the late 1800s when the population exploded.

But what made it even more popular was the way it was seen through the eyes of the artists who appreciated it. Renoir, Cézanne, Braque, and more have all painted popular works of art inspired by L'Estaque. There is even a self-guided walking tour marked by various plaques around the town that can help visitors see through the eyes of the artists themselves.

MARSEILLE TRAVEL GUIDE

Paul Cézanne may be the most famous artist to have glorified L'Estaque with the use of a paint brush. He first discovered the area in 1864 but came and went multiple times after that, including the time he returned in order to avoid being drafted to fight in the Franco-Prussian War.

There was one house that he always stayed at next to the church at Place Malterre. This location is now marked with a plaque and is visible as part of the self-guided walking tour. The image of L'Estaque that Cézanne tried to portray was that of a deep blue sea with plenty of red roofs looking down at it, always with plenty of light from the sun.

If you are in the area late in the summer, be sure to visit L'Estaque's annual festival, which takes place the first

MARSEILLE TRAVEL GUIDE

weekend in September. People come from all over to see their water jousting tournament.

L'Estaque can be easily reached by bus, metro, and train. From Marseille's Saint Charles Station, take the Blue Coast Train which makes regular stops. Or take the metro's line 2 toward Bougainville or tram line 2 to Joliette, then bus 35 to L'Estaque. Although it is easily accessible and now part of Marseille's 16th arrondissement, it has a completely distinguishable identity and atmosphere, making it well worth a visit.

Budget Tips

Accommodation

Hotel La Résidence du Vieux Port Marseille

18, Quai du Port

+33 491 91 9122

http://www.hotel-residence-marseille.com/

The Hotel La Résidence du Vieux Port Marseille was completely renovated in 2010 in the style of post-war modernism with tributes to Le Corbusier and Charlotte Perriand. It offers great sea views from most of its rooms as well as views of Basilica Notre Dame. Its lowest cost rooms offer a view of a quiet pedestrian street and cost 100 € per night. Breakfast is optional at an additional 18€ per night.

MARSEILLE TRAVEL GUIDE

Best Western La Joliette

49 Avenue Robert Schuman

+33 145 74 7672

http://www.hotel-joliette.com/

The Best Western La Joliette is a cozy, clean hotel located in a quiet neighborhood accessible by the Joliette metro station. It is situated in a convenient location near the Old Port and the Panier. Rooms have the vibe of a ship's cabin, but are designed elegantly in a way to pay homage to the rich shipping trade of the area. A typical room costs 189 €.

Music Hotel

12 Bld Salvator, 13006 Marseille, France

+33 491 02 1021

http://www.music-hotel.net/

The Music Hotel is a unique hotel with a contemporary theme and courteous staff. It is in a prime location within a 10 minute walk to the Vieux Port. Music Hotel offers free WiFi, large bathrooms with tubs, and optional breakfast for 10 € extra per person. Rooms start at 79 €.

MARSEILLE TRAVEL GUIDE

Hotel Lutia

31 Avenue du Prado

+33 491 17 7140

http://www.hotelutia.com/

The Hotel Lutia offers basic accommodations in a great location near the Old Port. Rates start as low as 47 € per night and include free WiFi. The owner is friendly and courteous.

Ibis Gare Saint Charles

Square Narvick

Esplanade Saint Charles

(+33) 491 95 6209

http://www.ibis.com/

The Ibis Marseille Gare Saint Charles is a 172 room hotel

with modern and convenient rooms that start at a rate of 71€ per night with free WiFi.

The hotel is within walking distance to the train station, Saint Charles. There is also a good restaurant on site.

🌐 Restaurants, Cafés & Bars

Although the Old Port is obviously the most populous in terms of dining choices, there are too many good restaurants to count in Marseille. Cours Julien is also a popular place to wander around until you find the right choice for your mood, as it is a pedestrian-only street with plenty of affordable restaurants and bars.

Four des Navettes

136 Rue Sainte,

+33 491 33 3212

MARSEILLE TRAVEL GUIDE

http://www.fourdesnavettes.com/fr/

Four des Navettes is a famous Marseille bakery located next to the St. Victor Fort. As the name states, it is famous for its navettes, which are a culinary specialty in the city. These dry, boat shaped biscuits are flavored with orange flower and orange zest. The bakery has been open since 1781 and the recipe has been kept secret for about a century.

Four des Navettes is open from 7 a.m. until 8 p.m. daily except for Sundays when it opens from 9 a.m. until 1 p.m. and again from 3 – 7:30 p.m.

L'Escapade Marseillaise

48 Rue Caisserie, behind the Hôtel de Ville

+33 491 31 6169

MARSEILLE TRAVEL GUIDE

L'Escapade Marseillaise is a favorite local hangout with typical Provençale cuisine and reasonable prices. It is open for lunch Mondays through Wednesdays from 11:30 – 2:30. On Thursdays through Saturdays, it reopens for dinner from 7:30 – 11:30. It is closed on Sundays.

Le Julien

114 Rue Paradis

+33 491 37 0622

http://www.lejulien.com/

Le Julien is a traditional French restaurant with reasonable prices as well as great food and ambiance. They also sell some of their products such as foie gras, chocolate, and wine baskets to take home as gifts. The restaurant is open for lunch Mondays through Fridays

MARSEILLE TRAVEL GUIDE

noon until 2: p.m., and dinner Tuesday through Saturday 7:30 p.m. until 10:30 p.m. Reservations are accepted.

The Cup of Tea

1 Rue Caisserie

+33 491 90 8402

This charming café is not only a place to stop for a spot of tea, but also a charming literary café. Indoors, you will find 50 varieties of tea as well as a library and exhibition space.

Outside sits a gorgeous terrace on which to sit and sip. The Cup of Tea is open from 8:30 a.m. until 7:00 p.m. Mondays through Fridays. On Saturdays, they open an hour later at 9:30 a.m. The restaurant is closed on Sundays.

La Brocéliande

9 rue Euthymènes

+33 491 54 3378

http://www.taverne-broceliande.com/

When in France, it would be a sin to avoid sampling a variety of crepes, the delicately thin pancake of the country. La Brocéliande is a traditional creperie and restaurant in the Old Port, offering a variety of French dishes at reasonable prices.

It is open Tuesdays through Fridays for lunch, from noon until 2:30 p.m. Dinner is served Tuesday through Thursday between 7:30 and 10:30 and on Fridays from 7 p.m. until midnight. On Saturdays, it is open from noon until midnight and on Sundays from noon until 10:30 p.m.

MARSEILLE TRAVEL GUIDE

🌐 Shopping

Le Centre Commercial les Puces

130 Chemin de la Madrague de la Ville

+33 491 58 5252

http://www.centrecommerciallespuces.com/

Le Centre Commercial les Puces is a large flea market in Marseille where you can find everything from fruit to antiques. With over 300 stalls, you are sure to find some unique items. It is open every day except Mondays from 8:30 a.m. until 7:30 p.m.

The Market at Noailles (Le Marché de Noailles)

Canebiere and Capucins

MARSEILLE TRAVEL GUIDE

If you go to any of the local markets that occupy Marseille, be sure to stop at the Market at Noailles, also known as the Marché des Capucins. It is located amongst the narrow streets that surround the top of the Canebière, just a short walk from the Old Port. This is the area around the Noailles subway station, which is one of the most interesting, diverse and colorful areas of the city.

The neighborhood hosts an Arabic and Indo-Chinese population which is reflected in the goods that are sold here. A walk through the market here could easily convince you that you are at a bazaar in Algeria. Although it is a bit crowded and chaotic, it is certainly colorful and great for both shopping and people watching.

Spices, rugs, African and Asian goods, as well as more traditional Provençal items can all be found here. It is open from 8 a.m. until 7 p.m. Mondays through Saturdays.

Prado Market

Avenue du Prado

The Prado Market is located along Avenue du Prado between the Castellane metro station and the Périer metro station. Here you can find a wide variety of clothing articles, specialty items, fruits and vegetables. On Friday mornings, there is also a flower market. The Prado Market is open daily between 8 a.m. and 1 p.m.

La Chocolatière du Panier

47 Rue du Petit Puits

+33 491 91 7970

http://lachocolatieredupanier.skyrock.com/

Satisfy your sweet tooth with some amazing and unique chocolate flavors at family-owned La Chocolatière du Panier. Here you can find a variety of unique chocolate treats in 300 different flavors that include onion and lavender, varying depending on what is in season at the time.

The chocolate shop is open on Mondays through Saturdays from 10 a.m. until 1 p.m. and then it reopens from 2:30 p.m. until 6:30 p.m.

Centre Bourse

17 Cours Belsunce

+33 491 14 0050

http://www.centre-bourse.com/30-8284-Accueil.php

Marseille's Bourse Shopping Center is the city's answer to

MARSEILLE TRAVEL GUIDE

a traditional shopping mall. With all of the street markets that dot the city, it really seems like a shame to spend your shopping experience indoors at a mall, but Centre Bourse offers a family-friendly shopping and entertainment experience if you want to avoid the hustle and bustle of the traditional street markets.

Centre Bourse is less than a five-minute walk from the Old Port and offers approximately 60 different shops and restaurants It is located in the safe area of Jardin des Vestiges, with three floors and a large mezzanine. If you are looking for brand names, this is probably the only place in Marseille where you will find them.

The Centre Bourse is very easy to find. If you are walking, simply head down the Canebiére, toward the Old Port.

MARSEILLE TRAVEL GUIDE

The entrance to the mall is on the right, across from Ironwood St.

The mall is open Mondays through Saturdays from 9:30 a.m. until 7:30 p.m.

MARSEILLE TRAVEL GUIDE

Know Before You Go

 Entry Requirements

By virtue of the Schengen agreement, visitors from other countries in the European Union will not need a visa when visiting France. Additionally Swiss visitors are also exempt. Visitors from certain other countries such as Andorra, Canada, the United Kingdom, Ireland, the Bahamas, Australia, the USA, Chile, Costa Rica, Croatia, El Salvador, Guatemala, Honduras, Israel, Malaysia, Mauritius, Monaco, Nicaragua, New Zealand, Panama, Paraguay, Saint Kitts and Nevis, San Marino, the Holy See, Seychelles, Taiwan and Japan do not need visas for a stay of less than 90 days. Visitors to France must be in possession of a valid passport that expires no sooner than three months after the intended stay. UK citizens will not need a visa to enter France. Visitors must provide proof of residence, financial support and the reason for their visit. If you wish to work or study in France, however, you will need a visa.

🌐 Health Insurance

Citizens of other EU countries are covered for emergency health care in France. UK residents, as well as visitors from Switzerland are covered by the European Health Insurance Card (EHIC), which can be applied for free of charge. Visitors from non-Schengen countries will need to show proof of private health insurance that is valid for the duration of their stay in France (that offers at least €37,500 coverage), as part of their visa application. A letter of coverage will need to be submitted to the French Embassy along with your visa application. American travellers will need to check whether their regular medical insurance covers international travel. No special vaccinations are required.

🌐 Travelling with Pets

France participates in the Pet Travel Scheme (PETS) which allows UK residents to travel with their pets without requiring quarantine upon re-entry. Certain conditions will need to be met. The animal will have to be microchipped and up to date on rabies vaccinations. In the case of dogs, France also requires vaccination against distemper. If travelling from another EU member country, you will need an EU pet passport. Regardless of the country, a Declaration of Non-Commercial Transport must be signed stating that you do not intend to sell your pet.

MARSEILLE TRAVEL GUIDE

A popular form of travel with pets between the UK and France is via the Eurotunnel, which has special facilities for owners travelling with pets. This includes dedicated pet exercise areas and complimentary dog waste bags. Transport of a pet via this medium costs €24. The Calais Terminal has a special Pet Reception Building. Pets travelling from the USA will need to be at least 12 weeks old and up to date on rabies vaccinations. Microchipping or some form of identification tattoo will also be required. If travelling from another country, do inquire about the specific entry requirements for your pet into France and also about re-entry requirements in your own country.

Airports

There are three airports near Paris where most international visitors arrive. The largest of these is **Charles De Gaulle** (CDG) airport, which serves as an important hub for both international and domestic carriers. It is located about 30km outside Paris and is well-connected to the city's rail network. Most trans-Atlantic flights arrive here. **Orly** (ORY) is the second largest and oldest airport serving Paris. It is located 18km south of the city and is connected to several public transport options including a bus service, shuttle service and Metro rail. Most of its arrivals and departures are to other destinations within Europe. **Aéroport de Paris-Beauvais-Tillé** (BVA), which lies in Tillé near Beauvais, about 80km outside

MARSEILLE TRAVEL GUIDE

Paris, is primarily used by Ryanair for its flights connecting Paris to Dublin, Shannon Glasgow and other cities.

There are several important regional airports. **Aéroport Nice Côte d'Azur** (NCE) is the 3rd busiest airport in France and serves as a gateway to the popular French Riviera. **Aéroport Lyon Saint-Exupéry** (LYS) lies 20km east of Lyon and serves as the main hub for connections to the French Alps and Provence. It is the 4th busiest airport of France. **Aéroport de Bordeaux** (BOD) served the region of Bordeaux. **Aéroport de Toulouse – Blagnac** (TLS), which lies 7km from Toulouse, provides access to the south-western part of France. **Aéroport de Strasbourg** (SXB), which lies 10km west of Strasbourg, served as a connection to Orly, Paris and Nice. **Aéroport de Marseille Provence** (MRS) is located in the town of Marignane, about 27km from Marseille and provides access to Provence and the French Riviera. **Aéroport Nantes Atlantique** (NTE) lies in Bouguenais, 8km from Nantes carriers and provides a gateway to the regions of Normandy and Brittany in the western part of France. **Aéroport de Lille** (LIL) is located near Lesquin and provides connections to the northern part of France.

Airlines

Air France is the national flag carrier of France and in 2003, it merged with KLM. The airline has a Flying Blue rewards

MARSEILLE TRAVEL GUIDE

program, which allows members to earn, accumulate and redeem Flying Blue Miles on any flights with Air France, KLM or any other Sky Team airline. This includes Aeroflot, Aerolineas Argentinas, AeroMexico, Air Europa, Alitalia, China Airlines, China Eastern, China Southern, Czech Airlines, Delta, Garuda Indonesia, Kenya Airways, Korean Air, Middle Eastern Airlines, Saudia, Tarom, Vietnam Airlines and Xiamen Airlines.

Air France operates several subsidiaries, including the low-cost Transavia.com France, Cityjet and Hop! It is also in partnership with Air Corsica. Other French airlines are Corsairfly and XL Airways France (formerly Star Airlines).

France's largest intercontinental airport, Charles de Gaulle serves as a hub for Air France, as well as its regional subsidiary, HOP!. It also functions as a European hub for Delta Airlines. Orly Airport, also in Paris, serves as the main hub for Air France's low cost subsidiary, Transavia, with 40 different destinations, including London, Madrid, Copenhagen, Moscow, Casablanca, Algiers, Amsterdam, Istanbul, Venice, Rome, Berlin and Athens. Aéroport de Marseille Provence (MRS) outside Marseille serves as a hub to the region for budget airlines such as EasyJet and Ryanair. Aéroport Nantes Atlantique serves as a French base for the Spanish budget airline, Volotea.

MARSEILLE TRAVEL GUIDE

🌐 Currency

France's currency is the Euro. It is issued in notes in denominations of €500, €200, €100, €50, €20, €10 and €5. Coins are issued in €2, €1, 50c, 20c, 10c, 5c, 2c and 1c.

🌐 Banking & ATMs

If your ATM card is compatible with the MasterCard/Cirrus or Visa/Plus networks and configured for a 4-digit PIN, you will have no problem drawing money in France. Most French ATMs have an English language option. Remember to inform your bank of your travel plans before you leave. Keep an eye open around French ATMs to avoid pickpockets or scammers.

🌐 Credit Cards

Credit cards are frequently used throughout France, not just in shops, but also to pay for metro tickets, parking tickets, and motorway tolls and even to make phone calls at phone booths. MasterCard and Visa are accepted by most vendors. American Express and Diners Club are also accepted by the more tourist oriented businesses. Credit cards issued in Europe are smart cards that that are fitted with a microchip and require a PIN for each transaction. This means that a few ticket machines, self-

MARSEILLE TRAVEL GUIDE

service vendors and other businesses may not be configured to accept the older magnetic strip credit cards.

🌐 Tourist Taxes

All visitors to France pay a compulsory city tax or tourist tax ("taxe de séjour"), which is payable at your accommodation. Children are exempt from tourist tax. The rate depends on the standard of accommodation, starting with €0.75 per night for cheaper establishments going up to €4, for the priciest options. Rates are, of course, subject to change.

🌐 Reclaiming VAT

If you are not from the European Union, you can claim back VAT (or Value Added Tax) paid on your purchases in France. The VAT rate in France is 20 percent on most goods, but restaurant goods, food, transport and medicine are charged at lower rates. VAT can be claimed back on purchases of over €175 from the same shop, provided that your stay in France does not exceed six months. Look for shops that display a "Tax Free" sign. The shop assistant must fill out a form for reclaiming VAT. When you submit it at the airport, you can expect your refund to be debited within 30 to 90 days to your credit card or bank account. It can also be sent by cheque.

MARSEILLE TRAVEL GUIDE

🌍 Tipping Policy

In French restaurants, a 15 percent service charge is added directly to your bill and itemized with the words *service compris* or "tip included". This is a legal requirement for taxation purposes. If the service was unusually good, a little extra will be appreciated. In an expensive restaurant where there is a coat check, you may add €1 per coat. In a few other situations, a tip will be appreciated. You can give an usherette in a theatre 50 cents to €1, give a porter €1 per bag for helping with your luggage or show your appreciation for a taxi driver with 5-10 percent over the fare. It is also customary to tip a hair dresser or a tour guide 10 percent.

🌍 Mobile Phones

Most EU countries, including France uses the GSM mobile service. This means that most UK phones and some US and Canadian phones and mobile devices will work in France. While you could check with your service provider about coverage before you leave, using your own service in roaming mode will involve additional costs. The alternative is to purchase a French SIM card to use during your stay in France. France has four mobile networks. They are Orange, SFR, Bouygues Telecom and Free. In France, foreigners are barred from applying for regular phone contract and the data rates are somewhat pricier on pre-paid phone services than in most European countries. You will need to show some form of identification, such as a passport when you make your purchase and it can take up to 48 hours to activate a French SIM card. If there is an Orange Boutique nearby, you can buy a SIM for €3.90. Otherwise, the Orange Holiday package is available for €39.99. Orange also sells a 4G device which enables your own portable Wi-Fi hotspot for €54.90. SFR offers a SIM card, simply known as le card for €9.99. Data rates begin at €5 for 20Mb.

Dialling Code

The international dialling code for France is +33.

Emergency Numbers

All emergencies: (by mobile) 112
Police: 17
Medical Assistance: 15
Fire and Accidents: 18
SOS All Emergencies (hearing assisted: 114)
Visa: 0800 90 11 79
MasterCard: 0800 90 13 87
American Express: 0800 83 28 20

Public Holidays

1 January: New Year's Day (Nouvel an / Jour de l'an / Premier de l'an)

MARSEILLE TRAVEL GUIDE

March - April: Easter Monday (Lundi de Pâques)

1 May: Labor Day (Fête du Travail / Fête des Travailleurs)

8 May: Victory in Europe Day (Fête de la Victoire)

May: Ascension Day (Ascension)

May: Whit Monday (Lundi de Pentecôte)

14 July: Bastille Day (Fête nationale)

15 August: Assumption of Mary (L'Assomption de Marie)

1 November: All Saints Day (La Toussaint)

11 November: Armistace Day (Armistice de 1918)

25 December: Christmas Day (Noël)

Good Friday and St Stephens Day (26 December) are observed only in Alsace and Moselle.

🌐 Time Zone

France falls in the Central European Time Zone. This can be calculated as Greenwich Mean Time/Co-ordinated Universal Time (GMT/UTC) +2; Eastern Standard Time (North America) -6; Pacific Standard Time (North America) -9.

🌐 Daylight Savings Time

Clocks are set forward one hour on the last Sunday of March and set back one hour on the last Sunday of October for Daylight Savings Time.

MARSEILLE TRAVEL GUIDE

🌐 School Holidays

The academic year in France is from the beginning of September to the end of June. The long summer holiday is from the beginning of July to the end of August. There are three shorter vacation periods. All schools break up for a two week break around Christmas and New Year. There are also two week breaks in February and April, but this varies per region, as French schools are divided into three zones, which take their winter and spring vacations at different times.

🌐 Driving Laws

The French drive on the ride hand side of the road. If you have a non-European driving licence, you will be able to use it in France, provided that the licence is valid and was issued in your country of residence before the date of your visa application. There are a few other provisions. The minimum driving age in France is 18. Your licence will need to be in French or alternately, you must carry a French translation of your driving permit with you.

In France, the speed limit depends on weather conditions. In dry weather, the speed limit is 130km per hour for highways, 110km per hour for 4-lane expressways and 90km per hour for 2 or 3-lane rural roads. In rainy weather, this is reduced to 110km, 100km and 80km per hour respectively. In foggy weather with poor visibility, the speed limit is 50km per hour on all roads. On urban roads, the speed limit is also 50km per hour.

By law, French drivers are obliged to carry a breathalyser in their vehicle, but these are available from most supermarkets, chemists and garages for €1. The legal limit is 0.05, but for new drivers who have had their licence for less than three years, it is 0.02. French motorways are called autorouts. It is illegal in France to use a mobile phone while driving, even if you have a headset.

🌐 Drinking Laws

The legal drinking age in France is 18. The drinking policy regarding public spaces will seem confusing to outsiders. Each municipal area imposes its own laws. In Paris, alcohol consumption is only permitted in licensed establishments. It is strictly forbidden in parks and public gardens.

🌐 Smoking Laws

From 2007, smoking has been banned in indoor spaces such as schools, government buildings, airports, offices and factories in France. The ban was extended in 2008 to hospitality venues such as restaurants, bars, cafes and casinos. French trains have been smoke free since December 2004.

MARSEILLE TRAVEL GUIDE

🌍 Electricity

Electricity: 220-240 volts

Frequency: 50 Hz

Electricity sockets in France are unlike those of any other country. They are hermaphroditic, meaning that they come equipped with both prongs and indents. When visiting from the UK, Ireland, the USA or even another European country, you will need a special type of adaptor to accommodate this. If travelling from the USA, you will also need a converter or step-down transformer to convert the current to to 110 volts, to avoid damage to your appliances. The latest models of many laptops, camcorders, mobile phones and digital cameras are dual-voltage with a built in converter.

🌍 Food & Drink

France is a paradise for dedicated food lovers and the country has a vast variety of well-known signature dishes. These include foie gras, bouillabaisse, escargots de Bourgogne, Coq au vin, Bœuf Bourguignon, quiche Lorraine and ratatouille. A great budget option is crêpes or pancakes. Favorite sweets and pastries include éclairs, macarons, mille-feuilles, crème brûlée and croissants.

The country is home to several world-famous wine-growing regions, including Alsace, Bordeaux, Bourgogne, Champagne,

Corse, Côtes du Rhône, Languedoc-Roussillon, Loire, Provence and Sud-Ouest and correctly matching food to complimentary wine choices is practically a science. Therein lies the key to enjoying wine as the French do. It accompanies the meal. Drinking wine when it is not lunch or dinner time is sure to mark you as a foreigner. Pastis and dry vermouth are popular aperitifs and favorite after-dinner digestifs include cognac, Armagnac, calvados and eaux de vie. The most popular French beer is Kronenbourg, which originates from a brewery that dates back to 1664.

Websites

http://www.rendezvousenfrance.com/

http://www.france.com/

http://www.francethisway.com/

http://www.france-voyage.com/en/

http://www.francewanderer.com/

http://wikitravel.org/en/France

http://www.bonjourlafrance.com/index.aspx

Made in United States
Orlando, FL
28 June 2023